A Spot

by Lucy Shepard
illustrated by Olivia Cole

Core Decodable 16

Bothell, WA • Chicago, IL • Columbus, OH • New York, NY

MHEonline.com

Copyright © 2015 McGraw-Hill Education

All rights reserved. No part of this publication may be reproduced or distributed in any form or by any means, or stored in a database or retrieval system, without the prior written consent of McGraw-Hill Education, including, but not limited to, network storage or transmission, or broadcast for distance learning.

Send all inquiries to:
McGraw-Hill Education
8787 Orion Place
Columbus, OH 43240

ISBN: 978-0-02-144797-8
MHID: 0-02-144797-7

Printed in the United States of America.

2 3 4 5 6 7 8 9 DOC 20 19 18 17 16 15

Mom has a pot.

Mom has a hot pot.
The hot pot tips!

Mom has a spot.

Dad has a mop.

Dad mops a spot.

Mom pats a spot.